D1288133

THE SEAWEED BOOK

How to Find and Have Fun with Seaweed

by
ROSE TREAT

Illustrated by
Laura Ford and James Sherrington

Photographs by Randy Duchaine

Star Bright Books
New York

Lower Macungie Library
3400 Brookside Road
Macungie, PA 18062

WITHDRAWN

For Joshua, Jeffrey, Julia, Alex, and Max

Copyright © 1995 Star Bright Books.
Text copyright © 1995, 1985 Rose Treat.
Published by Star Bright Books,
160 Broadway, New York, NY 10038.
All rights reserved. ISBN: 1-887734-00-7
(Previously 0-942820-15-0)
Library of Congress Catalog Card Number: 95-34391
Printed in Canada   10 9 8 7 6 5 4 3 2 1

This is a beginner's book about how to recognize some easily found seaweeds just as you recognize a daisy or a violet. It tells you how to find, collect, and preserve seaweeds so that you can have an ever-growing collection and can enjoy its amazing beauty forever.

Seaweeds grow on all coasts, except where there is too much ice for the plants to attach. You can find them on any visit to the seaside, growing on rocks or washed up on the shore.

By using a simple method of mounting, which is clearly explained and illustrated in this book, you can arrange seaweeds as easily as you would flowers in a bowl. You can use them to make a picture or to decorate cards. You can begin a scientific collection, or simply make a memento of a memorable day at the beach. The specimens shown in this book are just a beginning introduction to the beautiful seaweeds that can be found. By collecting them and other seaweeds that you find, you will add to your own delight and knowledge.

Although some seaweeds can be eaten, some are poisonous. Never put any seaweed in your mouth without first checking with an adult.

WHAT IS SEAWEED

Did you ever go to the seashore and see plants floating in to the beach? Did you ever see plants growing on rocks and seashells? Or plants lying on the beach?

These plants are seaweeds, and they are called marine algae. The word *algae* is Latin, and it means "water plants." Marine algae are saltwater plants. One plant is called an "alga."

Hundreds of different kinds of marine algae grow in salt water all around the world. They grow on rocks, on stones, on shells, on water animals, and on wood—the wood of wharves, bridges, and old shipwrecks. Some seaweeds even grow on other seaweeds. You will also find seaweeds lying on the beach drying in the sun.

Some kinds of seaweeds grow in deep water, some in shallow, some in places between high and low tides. Some grow in cold water, others in warm.

The more you look in different places, the more you will notice the different kinds of seaweeds—hundreds of different kinds.

Scientists have divided seaweeds into three main groups, according to color. If you want to know more about a particular seaweed that you have collected, you need to know which color group it belongs to. Then you can look the seaweed up in a seaweed reference book. The main color groups are:

Green algae
Brown algae
Red algae

When you pick up a particular seaweed, you may not always be able to tell right away which group it belongs to, because age and fading by the sun may change its color. For instance, green seaweeds sometimes become white when bleached by the sun.

Some seaweeds in the brown group may be black or yellow, yet they still belong in the brown group. Red seaweeds also vary in color and may be orange, pink, purple, or even white.

But after you have been collecting for a while, you will become more aware of the differences between the shape, size, color, and changed color of the seaweeds you find. And usually you will be able to tell what color group they belong to.

Seaweeds come in different shapes. They may look like heavy ropes, whips, threads, leaves, hands, feathers, or flower petals. Some have branches that fork, some have branches that mat together. Some have dense branches, some have sparse. Some branches are fine, some are thick. Some seaweeds are long and flat and have ruffled edges. Some are so thin that you can see right through them.

Seaweeds come in different sizes, too. Some kinds are so small you need a microscope to see them. Some are as tall as the tallest tree that you have ever seen.

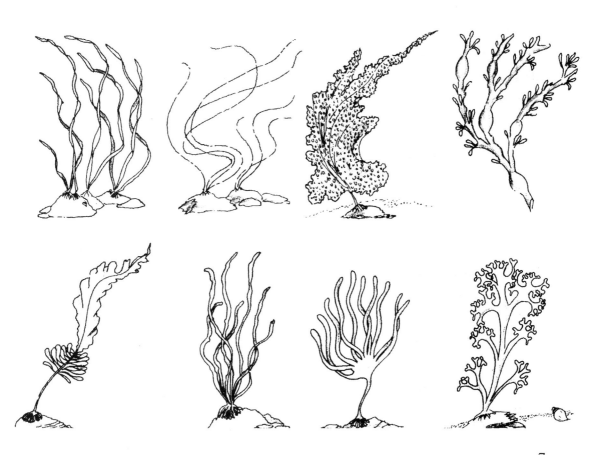

In some ways seaweeds are like land plants. They are home to some sea animals, just as trees and bushes are home for birds and some small animals. Sea plants are food for some fish and sea animals, just as land plants are food for some land animals.

Sea plants are hiding places for fish and sea animals and protect them from their enemies, just as bushes and trees protect land animals from their enemies.

But there are differences between land plants and sea plants. For example, seaweeds can only stand upright when supported by water. Land plants get their nourishment through their roots from the soil. Seaweeds get their nourishment from seawater. They don't have roots, they have grippers called "holdfasts." The only job the holdfast has is to keep the seaweed securely attached to an object in the water, such as a rock or a rusty anchor, despite the force of pounding waves.

Do you know that we use seaweed products almost every day? Maybe every day! Every time you use toothpaste, polish your shoes with shoe polish, or rub lotion on your body, you may be using a product that has seaweed in it.

Do you know that you eat seaweed almost every day? Look at the contents listed on the labels of ice cream and other dairy products, candy, puddings, and cookies, and you may find carrageen (*Chondrus crispus*) among them. A type of *Chondrus crispus* (page 18) is also called "Irish moss". In Ireland it is cooked with milk to make a pudding. Welsh people make "laver-bread" from *Porphyra* (page 16). And all over the world, people are discovering how delicious Japanese sushi and other foods made with seaweed taste.

Scientists have not paid as much attention to the study of seaweeds as they have to the study of land plants. There is still a lot to be discovered about seaweeds, such as which seaweeds different sea animals eat, how to grow various seaweeds, and in what new ways seaweeds can be used.

There is so much to find out. Perhaps you will be the person who will make important discoveries about seaweeds.

HOW TO COLLECT SEAWEED

This book shows several different kinds of seaweeds. You can find these and many other species in their particular habitats all over the world, except where there is too much ice for the holdfast to attach itself to an object.

The best place to look for seaweeds is along rocky shores, because seaweeds need an object for the holdfast to grip on to. The best time to look is during low tide, when you can pick seaweed where it grows. You can also find seaweeds along the tide line on a sandy beach. There you will often find seaweeds that rough seas have ripped loose during a storm. And for days after storms you can find seaweeds floating onto the shore.

When you collect seaweeds, use a plastic bag and put a small stone in it so that it doesn't blow away. Don't use glass jars or anything breakable. Pick up the seaweed where you see it floating or growing.

HOW TO PRESERVE SEAWEED

You can preserve your seaweed by mounting it on paper. This is how you do it. You will need:

- Heavy, stiff paper. (5" x 7" index cards are good to use)
- One toothpick
- One cotton ball
- Two bowls of water
- A towel or large white blotter

When you get home, put your collection in a bowl of water. Keep it out of the sun and keep it cool. Feel the seaweeds. They may feel slippery or leathery, stiff, stringy, or silky. Some seaweeds are very fragile and delicate. One kind is so fine it is called "mermaid's-hair." You will find a picture of it on page 25. Its scientific name is *Lyngbya*.

After putting your collection of seaweeds into a bowl of water, take a small piece of seaweed and put it all by itself into the second bowl of water. Watch it spread out.

If it is too bushy, pinch off some branches with your thumb and index fingernails and remove the scrap pieces from the basin. Specimens look better if they are well trimmed and thinned out.

Now you are ready to mount the seaweed.

Take an index card or a piece of heavy, stiff white paper and put it under the seaweed in the water. Hold the paper with one hand and hold the toothpick with the other. Use the tooth- pick to slide the seaweed onto the paper and to help spread it out. Carefully lift the paper with the seaweed on it out of the water.

If you want, you can poke the seaweed around with the toothpick to spread it out on the card. You can also use the cotton ball to drip water onto the seaweed on the card to spread it out even more.

Sometimes when you mount the seaweed you may see a shape, such as a cloud or a face. By pushing parts of the seaweed around with the toothpick, you can make a picture.

Next, put the mounting on a flat towel or large white blotter and leave it there until it dries.

Heavier seaweeds may need a different way of mounting. You can place a piece of heavy seaweed onto wet paper and then gently pour water on it to make it spread. Shape it by poking with a finger or a toothpick.

To dry such a specimen, put it on a white blotter or a clean cloth, like a towel or pillowcase or an old sheet cut to size. On top of the specimen place a layer of white netting curtain material, or you can use an old nylon stocking cut into a single layer. This prevents the seaweed from sticking to the second layer of white cloth, which you now put over the netting. This is like a sandwich, with the specimen in the middle.

Place a flat board on top of this pile and put weights, such as rocks or books, on the board. Change the cloths every day for two or three days, or until the specimen is dry.

Here is the order of placement for drying heavy seaweed: cloth, seaweed on paper, netting, cloth, board, rocks.

Seaweeds are covered with a natural glue called "mucin," so you will find that most seaweeds stick to the paper just as firmly as if they were glued on. If your seaweed hasn't stuck to the paper, use a white glue such as Elmer's or Sobo to attach it. Don't use rubber cement, as it may discolor the paper and the seaweed. Some seaweeds change color after they are dry.

Label your specimen, showing where and when you found it. For example: "Low tide, growing on rock in Clam Cove." Or, "Floating in water near Indian Rock, in Oyster Bay after heavy storm." Also write the date. Put it with your collection. Mounting and identifying seaweed gets easier to do after you have done it a few times.

You can store your mounted seaweeds in a looseleaf binder containing plastic sheet protectors.

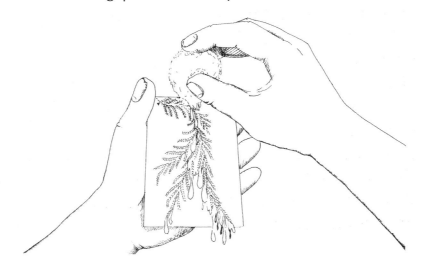

Your library has scientific reference books on seaweed, just as it has books on wildflowers and trees. You can check the names of many of your specimens. Keep the ones you cannot check until you find a friend or a teacher or a scientist who can help you.

Here are some examples of what you can make with mounted seaweed: bookmarks, birthday cards, Christmas cards, and personal notes. Dinner place cards made with seaweed are so charming that your guests will want to take them home.

The more you work with seaweed, the more beautiful objects you will create. Seaweeds are exquisitely beautiful, and no two are ever exactly alike.

IRISH MOSS PUDDING

*C*hondrus crispus is sometimes called "Irish moss." It can be bought in specialty stores and you can make a delicious pudding with it. It is easy to make. Ask a grown-up to help you with the cooking. Here is the recipe:

- About $1/2$ cup of Irish moss
- 1 quart of milk
- 1 teaspoonful of vanilla
- Pinch of nutmeg
- 1 tablespoon of sugar (or more to taste)

> Wash the seaweed very well to remove all the sand and other seaweeds or sea animals, that sometimes cling to it.
> Put the seaweed into a double boiler with the milk.
> Cook for $1/2$ hour.
> Strain the mixture into a bowl.
> Add the vanilla, the nutmeg, and the sugar to the bowl.
> Taste it. Add sugar if needed.
> Pour the mixture into a small dish or mold.
> Put in the refrigerator to chill it until firm.

Irish moss pudding is also called Blancmange

You can eat it plain, or it is delicious with crushed fruit such as strawberries, raspberries, or bananas.

On the following pages are photographs of some seaweeds that are easy to find. Make your own collection and keep adding to it whenever you are at the seashore.

PORPHYRA
pour-FY-ra

Porphyra is as thin as tissue paper. It is found mostly on rocks and wooden posts in the area between the high- and low-tide watermarks.

In Japan *Porphyra* is considered a delicacy and is especially grown near the seashore. The *Porphyra* farmer places a wooden post upright in the seabed and the seaweed grows onto it. The farmer weeds out other seaweeds just as you weed your garden. Every time you eat at an Asian restaurant, you most likely eat seaweed. Sushi is made with porphyra, which is called "nori" in Japanese.

This seaweed can be bought in specialty food stores.

Porphyra is a red alga, although sometimes it is purple or brown.

16

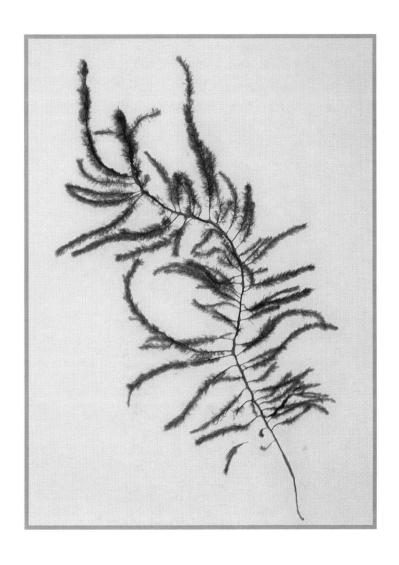

DASYA PEDICELLATA
DAY-zee-a   pe-DI-sell-AH-ta

This seaweed is mostly found in the month of August. It grows on shells and stones and is usually found at the low-tide watermark, and farther out in shallow, warm water. It has many branches. Along each branch are tiny, furry fringes. When this seaweed is taken from the water, it looks like a stringy wet rag.

This is a red alga. Sometimes it is slightly purple or brownish red.

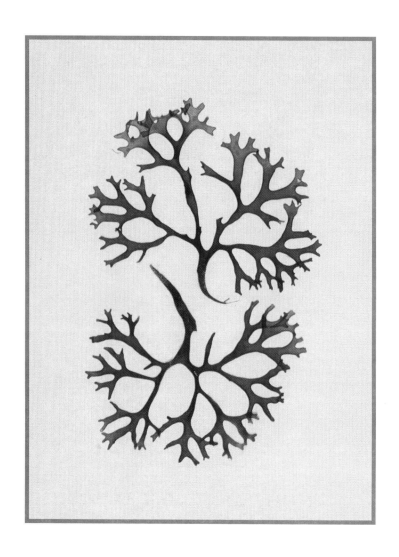

CHONDRUS CRISPUS
KON-drus KRIS-pus

This seaweed is commonly called "Irish moss." It grows on rocks between the high- and low-tide watermarks and is also found farther out at sea.

Chondrus crispus is one of the most important seaweeds. It is used in food, in medicines, and in scientific laboratories.

It is a red alga, although it may also be purple, yellow-green, or white. The sun bleaches this seaweed to a lighter color.

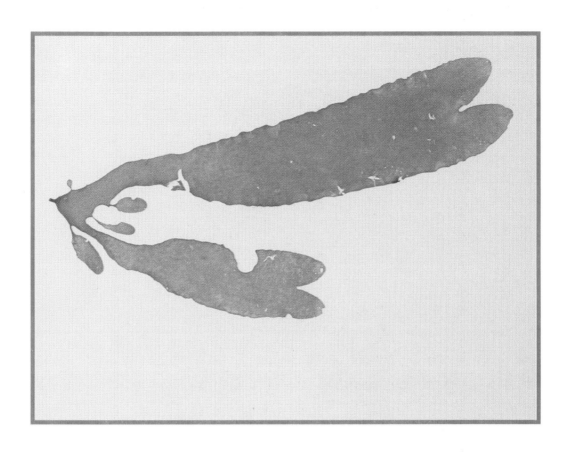

RHODYMENIA PALMATA
ro-DEE-MEAN-ee-a   pahl-MAH-ta

This seaweed is found in deep water. It grows on rocks and on other seaweeds. It looks like a hand with short, stubby fingers.

This seaweed has a very strong flavor, but some people find it tasty. It is also called "dulse," and it can be bought at specialty food stores.

It is a red alga. Sometimes it is purple.

GRINNELLIA AMERICANA
grin-EL-lee-a   a-MEH-ri-CAH-na

This seaweed grows in warm shallow water, farther out than the low-tide watermark. It grows on small shells and stones and can be as short as your little finger or as long as your arm. It is so thin, you can see right through it.

In August this seaweed can be found in bays and harbors.

This is a red alga. It is usually pink, but sometimes it is orange.

ECTOCARPUS
EK-toe-CAR-pus

This seaweed grows on other, larger seaweeds and on shells, rocks, and wood. It can be found all through the summer.

In the sea the branches of this seaweed look like feathers. The waves push them back and forth, just as a strong wind pushes the branches of a tree.

This is a brown alga. Sometimes it is olive green.

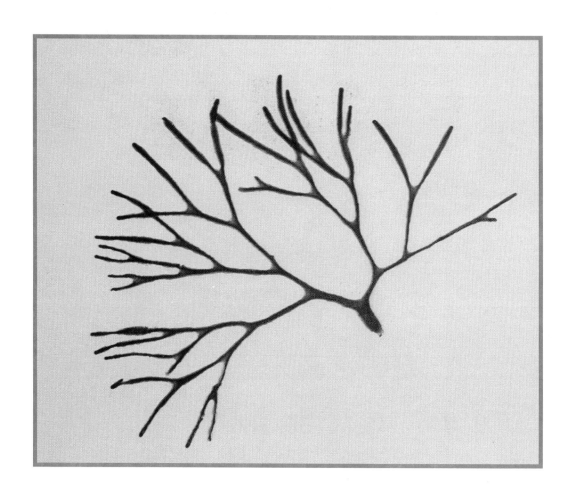

CODIUM FRAGILE
KO-dee-um   FRA-jee-lay

This is a very common seaweed. It grows on small stones and shells and is easy to find because there is so much of it.

It is very spongy and has puffed tips that keep it afloat. Sometimes, if this seaweed grows on an oyster, it will float away with the oyster attached. This makes oystermen unhappy because they lose many of their oysters this way.

It is a green alga.

CHORDARIA FLAGELLIFORMIS
kor-DAR-ree-a   FLA-jell-LEE-for-mis

This seaweed looks like a pony's tail. It grows on rocks and wood and can be found at low tide. It is often found growing beneath other seaweeds. It grows in large amounts and is very slippery.

This is a brown alga, although sometimes it is black.

DESMARESTIA VIRIDIS
DEZ-ma-RES-ti-a VIR-ree-dis

This seaweed grows on rocks just below the low-tide watermark and also farther out at sea. It can be found in late spring and early summer. It is easily recognized because it has a funny smell. It is a very bushy plant with branches that look like beautiful, long feathers.

When collecting this seaweed, keep it in a separate bag because if it is mixed with other seaweeds, it will rot them.

This is a brown alga. Sometimes it is olive green.

LYNGBYA
ling-BEE-A

This seaweed is sometimes called "mermaid's-hair" because it looks like very fine hair all tangled up. It is often found floating onto the shore in late summer.

Lyngbya is a poisonous seaweed and must not be eaten or put anywhere near your mouth.

It is a blue-green alga. Sometimes it is blackish green or blackish purple.

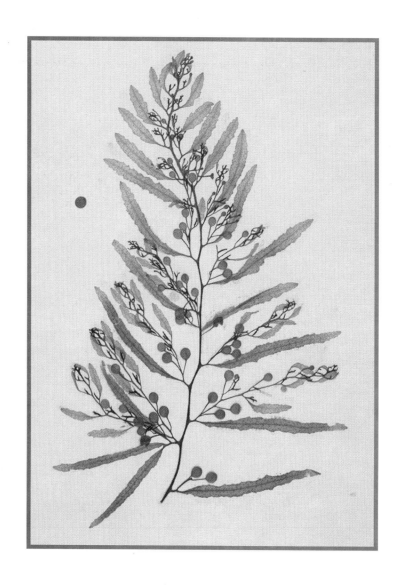

SARGASSUM FILIPENDULA
sar-GAS-um   FILL-lee-PEN-du-la

This seaweed grows on rocks and shells, just below the low-tide watermark and also farther out at sea. It can easily be distinguished from other seaweeds because it has stems and leaves.

Look at it carefully and you will see little puffed-up swellings. These small sacs are full of air and keep the plant upright in the water.

It is a brown alga. Sometimes it is greenish or yellowish brown.

FUCUS VESICULOSUS
FEW-kuss   ve-SICK-u-LOW-sus

This seaweed is called "rockweed." It is found between the high- and low-tide watermarks. It grows mostly on rocks and often covers the rocks on which it grows, but it also grows on wood and shells. It is very slippery so be careful when stepping on it.

Although it is sometimes greenish brown, it is a brown alga.

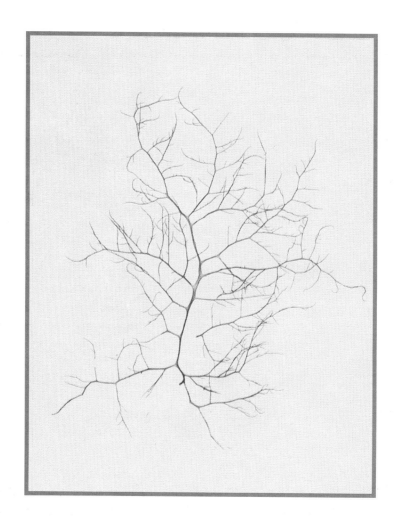

AGARDHIELLA TENERA
ah-GAR-dee-ella   ten-AIR-a

This alga grows on rocks and shells that lie in calm, shallow waters. It is a thick, rubbery, bushy plant. It can also be picked up from the sand. It can be found during spring, summer, autumn, and occasionally during winter.

Even though this is a thick, bushy plant, it can still be mounted. Simply cut a piece from the bush and mount it using the directions in this book (pages 11-13).

It appears in various shades of red, from deep red to pink. It is a red seaweed.

PHYCODRYS RUBENS
fy-KOD-rees   ROO-bens

This alga is one of the most beautiful of all seaweeds. It grows in deep water on stones, shells, and other alga. You will also find it on the seashore after a heavy storm.

This seaweed sticks easily to paper and is one of the many seaweeds that can be used to make holiday and greeting cards.

It is deep red to bright purple red. It is a red seaweed.

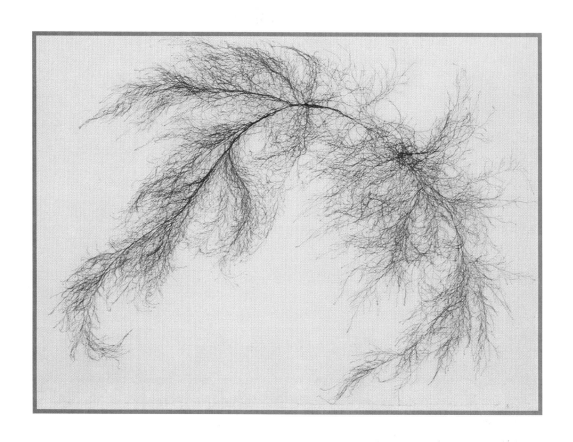

POLYSIPHONIA DENUDATA
POLLY-see-FOH-nee-a   DEN-oo-DAH-tah

This seaweed grows on stones, wood, and eelgrass (*Zostera*), and is found in bays that are protected from the harsh action of the ocean. Sometimes it can be found on the shore.

When mounting this seaweed, be careful, as the branches collapse when it is removed from the water. However, when it is floated onto paper, the branches will spread out.

It is reddish purple. It is a red seaweed.

SOME BOOKS ABOUT SEAWEED

Guberlet, Muriel Lewis
  Seaweed at Ebb Tide
  University of Washington Press, Seattle & London, 1956

Dawson, E. Yale
  How to Know the Seaweeds
  William C. Brown Co., Dubuque, Iowa, 1956

Dawson, E. Yale
  Seashore Plants of Northern California
  University of California Press, 1966

Chapman, V. J.
  Seaweeds and Their Uses
  Methuen & Co., Ltd., London, 1950

Kingsbury, John M.
  Seaweeds of Cape Cod and the Islands
  The Chatham Press, Inc., Chatham, Massachusetts, 1969

Taylor, William Randolph
  Marine Algae of the Northeastern Coast of North America
  Second Revised Edition
  The University of Michigan Press, Michigan, 1957

Parker, Steve
  Seashore (Eyewitness Books)
  Alfred A. Knopf, New York, 1989

photograph by Robert G. Tobey

Rose Treat was born in Czechoslovakia and never saw an ocean beach until she and her husband, mystery writer Lawrence Treat, rented a cottage on Martha's Vineyard.

On her first walk along the shore she became fascinated with the beauty of the seaweeds floating in the water, and she soon became an avid student and collector of seaweed. She regularly holds workshops for children and adults on the mounting of seaweeds.

Apart from being an avid student of phycology (study of seaweeds), Mrs. Treat is well-known as an amateur mycologist (student of wild mushrooms). Many of her photographs of wild mushrooms have won awards from the North American Mycological Association. Her mushroom slides are used in the Botany Department of Brigham Young University, Provo, Utah.

Seaweed, however, is the major creative force in Rose Treat's life, and she has developed an art form with this natural medium. Her seaweed collages have been exhibited at the Marine Biological Laboratory at Woods Hole, Massachusetts, Brooklyn Botanic Garden, Barnard College, Harvard University, and galleries in New England and New York. Her work is included in the permanent collections of the Marine Biological Laboratory at Woods Hole, the Vineyard Museum in Edgartown, Massachusetts, State University College at Potsdam, New York, and Harvard University. Rose Treat's seaweed mountings are also included in the Ocean Planet Exhibition of the Smithsonian Institution.